B *is for*
BAGEL

For Nina, Eli, and Ezra

Library of Congress Cataloging-in-Publication Data available.
ISBN: 978-1-951412-47-0
LCCN: 2021911088

Manufactured in China.

Photographs and food styling by Rebecca Wright.
Design by David Miles.
Some elements licensed from Shutterstock.com.

10 9 8 7 6 5 4 3 2 1

www.bisforbagel.com
Instagram: @bisforbagelbook
Facebook: @bisforbagel

The Collective Book Studio®
Oakland, California
www.thecollectivebook.studio

B is for BAGEL

RACHEL TEICHMAN

THE
collective
BOOK STUDIO

First,

knead the yeast and water
and the flour (but not too much).
Just push and pull the dough
until it's silky to the touch.

Now, let it rest and watch it as it
grows before your eyes.
Bit by bit it rises 'til it's
doubled up in size.

Roll out snakes of dough and make
some large (and squishy) rings.
Or roll a ball and poke a hole—
either of those things.

Splish! goes the water that is boiling in the pot.
Splash! go the bagels.
Watch out, it's very hot!

Remove them from the water
and then sprinkle each with seeds
(or another choice of flavoring
you think your bagel needs).

Now pop them in the oven;
your nose will smell them baking!
Be patient and don't rush,
no matter how long it's taking.

Ding! goes the timer.
Finally, they're here.
Delicious, homemade bagels
topped with butter, jam, or

. . . *schmear!*

A is for ASIAGO

cheesy, sharp, and creamy.

B is for **BLUEBERRY**

purple foods are dreamy.

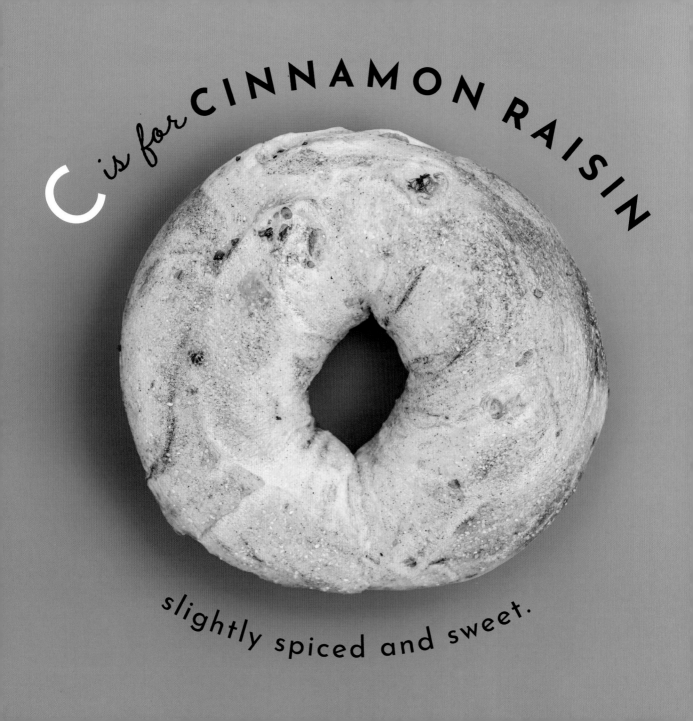

C is for CINNAMON RAISIN

slightly spiced and sweet.

D is for **DARK RYE**

with smoked fish, it's a treat.

E is for **EVERYTHING**

garlic, salt, and seeds.

F is for FRENCH TOAST

the start my morning needs.

G *is for* **GARLIC**

tangy, toasty, strong.

H is for **HEALTH GRAIN**

whole wheat is never wrong.

I is for ITALIAN

cheese and herbs, all diced.

J is for JALAPEÑO CHEDDAR

now that is very spiced!

K is for **KETTLE BOILED**

chewy from the pot.

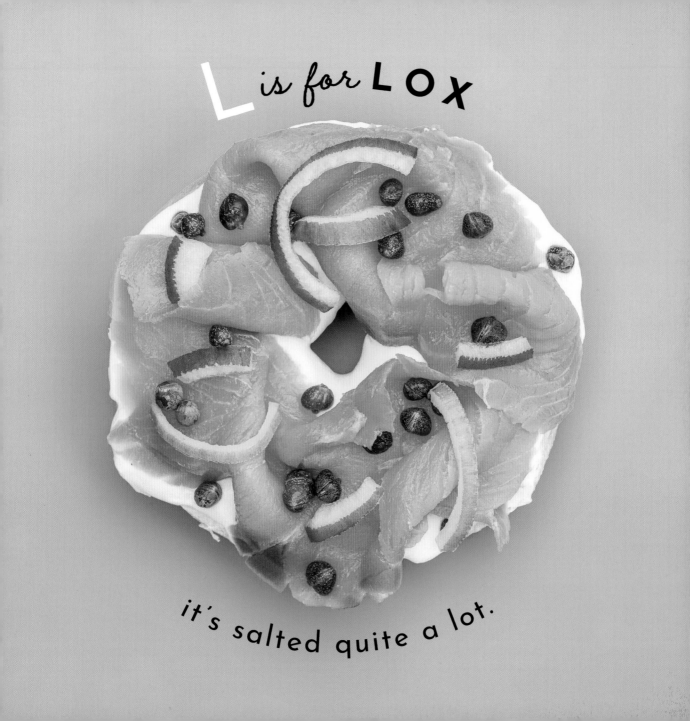

L *is for* **LOX**

it's salted quite a lot.

M is for MARBLE

swirly white and brown.

N is for NEW YORK PRETZEL

a salty taste of Midtown.

O is for **ONION**

those pungent little flakes.

P is for **POPPY SEED**

a few shakes is all it takes.

Q is for QUICK

it's yogurt mixed with flour.

R is for **RAINBOW**

the colors give it power!

S is for SESAME

a nutty, crunchy bite.

T is for **TOASTED**

whether wrong or right.

U is for **UNICORN**

it's magical and fun.

V is for VANILLA BERRY

a fruity taste of sun.

W is for **WHITEFISH SALAD**

such creamy smokiness.

X is for X·TRA SCHMEAR

don't ever make it less!

Y is for YEAST

it makes a bagel rise.

Z is for **ZA'ATAR**

try this one on for size.

From A to Z, our bagel friends
will be a tasty treat.
The only question that remains is . . .

Which one will *you* eat?

Traditional Bagels

Be sure an adult is on hand to help, especially with any boiling or baking.

For the dough

1 teaspoon active or instant dry yeast

1 tablespoon honey or sugar

¾ cup warm water (100°F to 109°F)

1 teaspoon salt

2 cups all-purpose flour

For the poaching liquid

6 cups water

1 tablespoon baking soda

1 teaspoon salt

Optional: 1 tablespoon honey or barley malt syrup

For the toppings (optional)

Sesame seeds

Poppy seeds

Dried onion

Dried garlic

Everything seasoning

Kosher salt

Cinnamon sugar

Sprinkles

TO MAKE THE DOUGH

1   In a small bowl, mix together the yeast, honey, and water and let sit for 10 minutes or until foamy.

2   In a large bowl, combine the flour and salt. Add the yeast mixture to the flour and mix until all of the flour is wet and the mixture is shaggy. Knead the dough in the bowl or on a floured work surface for 3 minutes.

3   Lightly oil a medium bowl. Place the ball of dough in the bowl, cover with a warm damp cloth, and place it in a warm, dry area to rise for 1 hour.

4   Line a baking sheet with parchment paper. Fill a small bowl with water.

5   Turn the dough out onto a lightly floured work surface and, using a knife or a bench scraper, cut the dough into 4 equal pieces for regular-size bagels, or into 12 equal pieces to make mini bagels. Roll each piece of dough into a 6-inch or 4-inch rope, depending on the size bagel you are making. Wet one end of a dough rope with just a little bit of water and form it into a circle, pressing the ends together firmly to seal them. The water will help them stick. (Another option is to roll each piece of dough into a ball and poke a hole through it with your finger.) Repeat with the rest of the dough ropes. Place the dough circles on the prepared baking sheet and set aside for about 10 minutes at room temperature.

TO MAKE THE POACHING LIQUID

6   Preheat the oven to 400°F. Place an oven rack in the top third of the oven.

7   In a large saucepan, mix together the water, baking soda, and salt and bring to a boil over high heat, stirring to dissolve the baking soda and salt. Lower the heat until the water is just gently boiling, about medium-low. Drop the bagels into the water, 1 or 2 at a time, depending on the size, and boil for 30 seconds for mini bagels or 45 seconds for regular-size bagels. Flip the bagels over and repeat the boiling time. Using a slotted spoon, transfer the bagels to the baking sheet. Immediately add any desired toppings to the bagels (while they are still wet).

8   Bake in the top third of the oven for 10 to 12 minutes, flipping them halfway if they get too brown. Remove from the oven and let cool on a wire rack. Store in an airtight container or bag for several days, or freeze.

Quick Bagels

While this is not an authentic bagel recipe and the flavor and texture is not the same, it is an opportunity for kids to try out making bagels easily. This recipe eliminates the need for rising and boiling, making it a much quicker process. Be sure an adult is on hand to help!

For the dough

2 cups self-rising flour or 2 cups flour + 2 teaspoons baking powder + ½ teaspoon salt

1 cup nonfat Greek yogurt

1 egg

1 tablespoon water, plus more if needed

For the egg wash

1 egg

1 tablespoon water

For the toppings (optional)

Sesame seeds

Poppy seeds

Dried onion

Dried garlic

Everything seasoning

Kosher salt

Cinnamon sugar

Sprinkles

TO MAKE THE BAGELS

1. Preheat the oven to 350°F. Line a baking sheet with parchment paper.

2. In a large bowl, mix together the flour, yogurt, and egg until well combined. Add more flour, a little at a time, if the dough is too soft. If the dough is too stiff, add 1 tablespoon of water and mix until well combined. It should feel soft and not too stiff, like a dough you could play with.

3. Place the dough on a clean work surface and divide the dough into 4 equal pieces for large bagels or 8 pieces for mini bagels. Roll each piece of dough into a 6-inch snake for large bagels or a 4-inch snake for mini bagels. Wrap one of the dough snakes around your fingers to form a circle and pinch the ends together firmly. You can stretch the ring out a little to try to keep the hole from closing while baking. Place the formed dough onto the baking sheet. Repeat with the rest of the dough pieces.

4. In a small bowl, mix together the remaining egg and 1 tablespoon of water. Lightly brush the bagel tops with the egg mixture. Sprinkle on your desired toppings.

5. Bake for 25 minutes, or until the bagels are browned. Remove from the oven and let cool on a wire rack. Store in an airtight container or bag for several days, or freeze.

About the Author

Rachel Teichman is a freelance writer who covers cooking and crafting ideas for families as well as local finds. She created Crafts and Crumbs to share her favorites on social media (@craftsandcrumbs). Her work has appeared in *The Buzz Magazines*, *Kveller*, and *Red Tricycle*. She has lived all over the United States and now resides with her husband and three children in Houston, Texas, where the bagels are excellent. Her favorite bagel is whole wheat with scallion cream cheese.

Acknowledgments

Rebecca Wright, for wrangling sunlight, cats, and bagels.

The Collective Book Studio—Angela, David, Elisabeth, AJ, Amy, Dean, and Ella—for doing what you love so well.

The Bagel Shop Bakery, for all of the support and bagels you have given to this project and to the Houston community.

Riana and Michael, for sharing your love of books and bagels.

Like Minds Communications, for making me a #bagelinfluencer.

Proof Home Bakery, for making the quick bagels happen.

The rest of the local bagel community for your support (and bagels).

Emily, for mailing me some from D.C. to complete the alphabet.

My friends, for "everything," and for helping to eat a bajillion bagels.

My whole family coast to coast, for many shared bagel brunches.

My dad, who fills our house with books.

My mom, who taught me that it was ok to be a bagel snob.

Jesse, love you a lox.